WORLD FAMO[US] ROUND HER[E]

◆

The Photographs of Jack Hulme

WORLD FAMOUS ROUND HERE

◆

The Photographs of Jack Hulme

Edited by

RICHARD VAN RIEL

OLIVE FOWLER

HARRY MALKIN

Introduction

STEPHEN McCLARENCE

Foreword

COLIN FORD

Head of National Museum of Television, Film and Photography

YORKSHIRE ART CIRCUS
in association with
WAKEFIELD METROPOLITAN DISTRICT COUNCIL
1990

Published by
Yorkshire Art Circus
School Lane, Glass Houghton, Castleford

© Yorkshire Art Circus
© *Design:* Kevin Reynolds & Wayne Clarida of Underline Laser Graphics
© *Photographs:* Jack Hulme
© *Frontispiece and Back Cover Photograph:* Stephen McClarence
© *Introduction:* Stephen McClarence
Yorkshire Art Circus is grateful for the support of West Yorkshire Grants and Yorkshire Arts

Photographs processed by
Berris Connolly

Typeset by
Underline, Stuart House, St Andrews Court, Leeds

Printed by
FM Repro Ltd, 69 Lumb Lane, Roberttown, West Yorkshire

ISBN 0 947780 57 2

Sponsors
AMEC Regeneration Ltd
Marks and Spencer PLC
The Graham Poulter Partnership PLC

Editorial Team
Margaret Edwards
Christine Moorsby
Rachel Van Riel
Tony Lumb
Brian Lewis
Lillian Whiteley
Janet Spears
Ian Clayton
Rachel Adam

FOREWORD

THERE is a strong tradition of documentary photography in England and part of the tradition is that all documentary photographers quickly make their way to the gritty North. Gleefully, they jump on a train at King's Cross or Euston, eager to search out bleak industrial ruins and penniless unemployed workers. Even those born in the North sometimes fall into the trap, contributing to an image that is as fake and as partial as the stereotyped portraits once churned out by High Street Studios.

In truth, the best portraits are often taken by our nearest and dearest – who need to know no more about photography than which button to press, and which chemist's shop makes the best prints.

Jack Hulme's portrait of Fryston is that of a true insider, familiar, intimate, knowing. Those who lived there clearly trusted him, and faced his camera with pride. He repaid that trust by recording their way of life, at work and at play, simply, honestly, and with love.

Let me come clean. Though Yorkshire has made me feel very much at home, I was born a Southerner. So I can only regret the fact that I never had the privilege of seeing one of Jack Hulme's paraffin-lit magic lantern shows, nor meeting my wife in the local flea pit, nor participating in any of the events shown in this book. It is my loss. Jack makes his village seem like the best place on earth to have lived. In one sense of the word, Fryston – built to house miners in a colliery which is now closed – is dead. In another, thanks to Jack, it will live forever.

COLIN FORD, HEAD OF MUSEUM, NATIONAL MUSEUM OF PHOTOGRAPHY, FILM & TELEVISION, BRADFORD

INTRODUCTION

FAME came late in life for Jack Hulme. But he was ready for it. In his early eighties he welcomed journalist after journalist, film crew after film crew, to his terraced house in Fryston, a pit village two miles North East of Castleford in West Yorkshire. The visitors never had any difficulty finding the house. A hand-painted plaque alongside the front door proclaimed 'Jack Hulme, 7 North Street.'

It was that sense of confident self-identity that had made possible the amazing story Jack told his interviewers – of how he was born and had spent all his life in this village and had photographed it over a period of 60 years. A miner himself, he had covered the 1926 strike and its 1984 sequel. He had captured the village in its heyday, with 1,300 working at the pit, and had chronicled its decline to a community of around 100. Fryston Colliery closed in 1985 and when the pithead gear was demolished late in 1987, Jack was there with his camera. He had spent over half a century photographing one square mile of one village – a concentration perhaps unique in photographic history.

He stored his negatives in wallets and rusting toffee tins. Many deteriorated, some of the early glass plates were smashed, and Jack thought little about his collection until 1985 when Yorkshire Art Circus appealed for photographs for a book of 'local voices.' He sent off half a dozen pictures – so good that they prompted a casual request for more. 'I've got 10,000 more in the attic if that's any help,' he said.

The pictures he brought down were a treasure trove. The Art Circus staged an exhibition of the best of them at Pontefract Museum in 1986. It pulled in 10,000 visitors. They have subsequently been exhibited all over Britain, have gone on show in Europe, have inspired a play, and have generated immense media interest.

Jack Hulme enjoyed four years of this celebrity before he died in January 1990 at the age of 83. At his funeral service, mourners in the corrugated iron village chapel heard him described simply as 'Mr Fryston.' It was a role he enjoyed. He considered himself 'a bloke who'd do owt for anybody' and often talked of himself in the third person.

As miner, leader of the village harmonica band, and barber, he was known to everyone in Fryston. And as the village's semi-official photographer, he turned up at most functions and could be relied upon for passport portraits. When Fryston couples got married, they asked Jack to take the photographs – many of his negatives feature wedding groups from six decades. The babies he photographed in the 1930s became grandparents – and then he photographed them again.

These formal portraits, some posed in front of

a Parisian backdrop bought in Blackpool, are generally effective. But it is Jack's other photographs which are so remarkable – a moving documentary record of everyday life in one village, an insider's view of his own community. 'There was always something to photograph,' he said. 'I took them for pleasure; I got nothing for it.'

Most photographs of working class life are taken by outsiders - voyeuristic intruders who poke around with their lenses and move on to the next project. Jack lived the way of life he photographed. With rare insight, sympathy and humour, his pictures show a warm, vigorous, tightly-knit community typical of industrial Northern England. He photographed the big village events – the VE Day and Coronation celebrations, the annual charabanc trips, retirements, football teams. He photographed the annual Fryston Carnival and pinned up his pictures in the draper's window, for sale for a few pence. He followed the expansion and decline of the pit – through the opening of the pit head baths in 1932, nationalisation in 1948, and the building of the Miners' Welfare in 1952 – though even during the pit's decline there was no strong political dimension to his work. He preserved the memory of a dying community, but to the end retained an unshakeable conviction in the justice of 'the circumstances of the moving world.'

With unflagging enthusiasm he – perhaps most

valuably – photographed the 'mundane,' the ordinary, unexceptional fabric of community life – the streets, the pubs, the Home and Colonial Stores, the allotments, pea-picking, women donkey-stoning their front steps or black leading their fireplaces, children playing or washing in a tin bowl in the kitchen sink, groups of men sitting and talking on the pavement. They are the pictures most other amateur photographers rarely take – except for granted. 'Who'd think of taking that?' he would ask as he sorted through his negatives. 'Not one in a hundred! I took a lot of pictures other people wouldn't even bother with because they wouldn't think the subjects were important enough.' He even reputedly photographed his own wife's funeral, though the negatives have not survived.

Jack was trusted by the people he photographed. He was familiar enough for his camera to be almost unnoticed. So his pictures are for the most part intimate, unposed and unselfconscious. They show his friends and neighbours as they informally were, rather than as they might have posed for posterity. He gave them copies of the pictures – so where most family albums are full merely of weddings, christenings and holidays, Fryston family albums are a rich archive of the everyday life that can so easily go unrecorded. Jack had an uncanny instinct for making the ordinary memorable – as a celebration of the present rather than a systematic archive for the future. They remain a precious document, holding a key to their community's identity. They have given the people of Fryston a sense of place, a sense of belonging, a context. 'You know that picture Jack took in the Forties of lads jumping off a bridge?' says a man approaching retirement. 'Well, I'm third from the left.'

Few collections of photographs have such value as social history, though it would be wrong to imagine they have no further aesthetic worth. Some explore a gentle surrealism – Jack's own mother asleep on her couch with floral wallpaper blooming dreamily around her, a woman in her best summer frock sitting in a field with a gas mask on her head, a lone fiddler stumbling on his crutches with his violin hung round his neck.

The pictures are given an added poignancy by Fryston's curiously enclosed geography. Built specifically to house the Victorian pit's miners, it was sandwiched between the River Aire and the colliery railway line, with only one approach road over a narrow railway bridge. Self-contained and largely self-sufficient, it was often likened to one big interdependent family, with a sometimes claustrophobic feeling of physical and social isolation communicated strongly in the pictures. The village revolved around the pit. It shrank a little when the back-to-backs were bulldozed in the 1950s, and shrank more drastically in the early 1980s as the pit was run-down. A dozen brick terraces were reduced to three, most of the villagers moved away, and the houses that remained – including Jack Hulme's home for the last 46 years of his life – overlooked a bleak wasteland.

Today the site of the pit is a desolate brick-strewn prairie. The bus service to Castleford has been withdrawn and the village has no reason for being there any more. To walk round Fryston is to walk round a ghost village. Carthorses graze in the fields, miners walk their whippets and neighbours gossip on their doorsteps, as they did half a century ago in Jack Hulme's pictures. Coal pickers sift handfuls of muck and drop slivers of coal into sacks slung over their bicycle handlebars. A strange silence haunts the place, with time curiously suspended. Lupins bloom among the twisted wires poking from the ground; children's voices echo from estates two miles away; chirping birds can be heard for the first time in 110 years. It is a scene almost inconceivably remote from the thriving community of Jack's photographs. 'You wonder where they put it all,' says one of the survivors, passing the site of the school, the chapel and the pit head baths. The old way of life has gone forever. 'I feel a little bit sick of heart,' Jack remarked in 1988. 'I've been robbed of something I've always lived with.'

Jack Hulme had a great enthusiasm for the technical aspects of photography. He loved 'gadgets' and bought a television and a video when they were still novelties. He was, he once boasted, the first person in Fryston to own a microwave. He bought his first camera in 1920 at the age of 14 – a second-hand Box Brownie costing half-a-crown, with a few glass plates thrown in. With it he took unerringly sensitive studies of his mother and, as he said, 'soon found that a man with a camera was always popular with the girls. They would always be knocking on our door saying "Come on Jack and take our photos."'

He graduated from glass plates to 120 film – and a camera for which he saved up stamps in John Bull magazine. Eventually, and most successfully, he moved into 35 mm. In 1941, his first wife Lydia saved £91 – then a vast sum - to buy him a Leica camera. 'It was in a class of its own,' he said. 'I never missed a shot.' He was as proud of the camera as he was scornful of equipment he regarded as outmoded. He recalled a press photographer he met: 'He had a plate camera and I said "That's no bloody good. I've got a Leica." He had a great big flash unit – like carrying a coal scuttle around.' Jack took many of his best pictures with the Leica, composing the images in the frame, sometimes using outdated RAF film, processing in the pantry and printing with an enlarger made from a vacuum cleaner. Later, when his eyesight started to fail, he bought an automatic camera and moved into colour. His enthusiasm never flagged.

Even when confined to his bed, he took photographs of his dog watching the television.

Jack said he felt humbled by all the fuss his pictures had caused. He had never considered them worthy of attention. But he rapidly grew to enjoy his celebrity and always rose to the occasion. One of the last TV documentaries about him was filmed six months before he died. Though very weak and tired, he insisted on taking part and sat waiting in the downstairs back room where he had slept for the past four years, with the list of his tablets pinned to the wall next to his bed. The film crew doubted whether he was up to an interview, but the moment the camera lights were switched on, Jack summoned his old energy and gave a resiliently cheerful performance. 'I know what you want,' he told the TV researcher. 'You want Jack Hulme's autograph.'

A couple of years before he died, Jack was himself being photographed outside his home. A passer-by looked quizzically on. 'It's all right,' Jack explained. 'I'm Jack Hulme. I'm famous, you know. World famous round here.'

STEPHEN McCLARENCE

The stories which appear in WORLD FAMOUS ROUND HERE have been collected through interviews with current and ex-residents of Fryston. Yorkshire Art Circus would like to thank everyone who generously gave the time to share their memories.

Whilst the stories in this book are about real characters and events in Fryston, we must point out that the text adjoining each photograph does not necessarily refer directly to the people appearing in it.

OUR houses were back-to-back and at the time were said to be the best houses in Europe. We had one big room downstairs, two bedrooms, a cellar and an attic; plenty of room for a big family.

Wonderful times. During the war, people tended to stick together, you never locked your doors. Everybody went into each other's houses, there was no stealing – a few rows maybe, but they soon blew over and everyone was friends again. Anyone in trouble would always be helped out, be it food or money. The war created neighbourhoods.

MY dad encouraged me in photography and music. When I was nine he bought me a Box Brownie.

I used to go taking my own pictures and he developed them. When I was seventeen he bought me a camera in a sale at Woolworths for 25/-. It got lost after I left it at my mate's. It turned up years later but by then I couldn't get films to fit it.

I suppose my photography took second place to learning the piano really but even then Dad wanted his say.

He used to frighten me to death; he didn't know how to play the piano himself but he'd sit in the other room shouting, 'Wrong note, wrong note!' He was very strict.

As kids we used to sit on that wall watching Cuddy Bateson sticking pigs and felling them.

He did it just next to the wall. Cuddy used to hold the pigs steady with a rope and as soon as the head was steady his mate Billy would stun it with his hammer.

He had a tool with a hammer on one side and a metal spike on the other; after he'd stunned it he'd turn it round and whack it with the spike, right on the forehead. Then it went straight into the bath of boiling hot water to be scraped down.

After that he'd hang the pig up in a doorhole with a piece of ash wood through its back legs, pull the trotters off with a hook and cut them from between the legs straight up so the guts fell out. He used to let the blood run into his drinking pot and then have a sup of it while it was still warm.

We'd be waiting eagerly for the bladder so we could use it as a football and he'd just chuck it at us. It would still be full of pee so we'd nick it with a blade, empty it and then it would be good for three or four games of football. A bladder had layers of skin and one came off during each game.

Cuddy was found dead in the quarry. He'd killed himself with his own boning knife.

EVERYONE decorated their houses for VE day. There was competition of course but it was friendly. Some people went to elaborate lengths to make their house the best in the street – Union Jacks, strings of flags, painted bricks, the lot.

THERE were two Lillians in our class, me and Lillian Baines. She was a very pretty little girl and as an only child she was very nicely dressed and always wore a big satin bow in her hair to match the colour of her dress. I was different; thin with a severe Joan of Arc haircut.

This morning when the teacher marked the register she called out our names alphabetically. Lillian Baines answered 'Yes miss' to her name. When it came to my turn to respond the teacher looked up from the register and directly at me. 'We can't have two Lillians in class, it will cause too much confusion. Lillian Owen, we shall call you Lily.'

'Miss, my name's Lillian not Lily,' I said very near to tears. At this she turned bright pink and gave me a good telling off for being insolent. I refused to answer to the shortened version of my name for several days but I had to give in in the end.

It wasn't until I grew up that I realised that was the day when I had my first experience of class distinction.

MY dad was a Conservative until Maggie Thatcher came along. My Aunt May would say, 'The Conservatives know about money and will look after yours for you.' I wasn't so sure about that.

Of course you have to remember that Fryston was a funny place and in general politics was hush-hush. It was a different world, shut off if you like. When I left school Rose wanted to fix me up in the little village shop. They considered I travelled a lot because I worked in Pontefract, five miles away. Airedale was right next door but many wouldn't entertain people from Airedale.

THERE were always horses in the streets but I have to say that my only experience of mounting one was at Bridlington.

What I remember most is when I was up there it suddenly decided to do a wee and there I was sitting with everybody watching me as the steam rose higher and higher.

THE Fryston Home Guard provided a few laughs. The leader once got them all together, said 'Follow me!' and then marched his men straight into the river.

We had a sten gun and we'd all go up to the lime quarry to watch Popsie Gray have target practice. He'd set tin cans on rocks and fire the sten gun but it was so powerful that the recoil would send the barrel of the gun up in the air and there would be bullets flying all over. We had to scatter or we'd all have been shot.

One day during the war the alarm went up that a German paratrooper had landed in the Welfare. They got all the Home Guard together and Mr Bullock gave the order, 'Don't tackle him, he might have a gun!' They skirted round and saw a white heap in the middle of the cricket pitch. When Mr Bullock saw it he shouted, 'You blind bleeder, it's Harry Pick's white horse!'

THEY call it gurning up in Cumberland and push their heads through a lavatory seat to do it but here they just take out their teeth and call it pulling faces.

The world champion gurner, I do believe, was Mr Nutter of Kells.

O F rugby they sometimes say, 'He talks a good game,' and of pigeons they say, 'He talks a good race'.

It was all pigeons in them days. They would bet on anything though usually they raced for cups and honour not for big money. This is a picture of Joe Payne and his cousin Chunner. I don't know why he was Chunner but most men had special features. Most pits had a 'Donkey Dick.'

I remember Mother going with her basket just as the stalls were closing. She had a basket full of food for two and sixpence. We would sit round the fire with a plate with half an apple, half an orange and some boiled sweets and broken biscuits.

We never had a whole Easter egg. She always said she had dropped them but as they were a mixture of dark and light chocolate we were always puzzled.

JACK spent hours on end watching them building the stadium at Fryston. On the opening day they started off with a Brass Band, then parades of Boy Scouts and Girls' Life Brigade and Yugoslavian dancers in national dress with their own band, and they were real Yugoslavians, mind.

My aunt was in charge of putting her brothers and sisters to bed as a kid and she hated the job.

She wasn't allowed to leave them until they were asleep. She used to blow on their eyes to make them shut them and shout, 'They're asleep, Mother.' She was sick of babies, always more babies every year.

THE Home and Colonial was in Carlton Street, Castleford. It was very special. Sometimes you could get their tin biscuit boxes for use in the house. You stored things in them.

Do you remember the meat safes with wire gauze on them that we had before refrigerators? They made lovely cages for ferrets.

MINING was a reserved occupation so lots of men stayed in the village during the war. On VE Day, for a bit of a laugh, the men put on pinafores and started serving. They wouldn't have done that on a normal day but then VE Day weren't normal.

My dad could always make us laugh. On Sundays he'd get a little brass shovel full of coal and say, 'Come on we'll give the pigs their Sunday tea.'

Pigs used to like crunching slack coal and it was better bacon then as well.

I didn't get married because of looking after my parents, but I did meet a lot of men in the forces.

When you were courting you went to the pictures mostly, or to a dance. You used to go for walks and you were invited out to tea. They weren't boyfriends, you'd call them young men in those days.

THERE were seven of us kids in the family. We had to pick a bag of coal before we went to school and then we got the cane because we had dirty hands.

We always had bread and jam for breakfast and in the morning part of school we had to have a big spoonful of cod liver oil. Then at dinner we used to race home like mad to see who got the first lot of chips out of the pan that my mam had made.

On the day the Mayor came to our school we all had to be scrubbed and clean specially for the occasion.

THAT'S Teddy Matthews and his roller. If you look down the street there's the Wesleyan Chapel and opposite it is where Harry Pickersgill used to sit taking bets.

In those days Fryston men would bet on anything. I've seen them bet a pint for a man that someone wouldn't dive into the Aire and swim under the Tommy Puddings and come out the other side.

Every village had a bookie taking bets on the horses and dogs. The only legal way to bet was to use a licenced betting office but there was always a few bookies' runners in the club or down by the toilets.

They had to be careful of the local bobby as he was always after them. Eventually Harry opened an office in a big blue hut but he still used runners. Most bets were paid out on starting prices from the course and when Harry ran out of paper, he'd chalk the results on the lavatory's sloping roof for all to see. Harry made his pile before he sold out to the big boys.

IF we stayed at home poorly as kids, Mother always put extra snap in Dad's tin, so that when he got back from the pit we could have the left over as a treat. Sandwiches always tasted nicer out of a snap tin.

Mother used to make what she called Shouting Cake. You shouted if you found a currant.

IF you met a woman on the way to work you turned round and went back home because it was unlucky.

The pubs were full of pitmen on Monday afternoons when they would knock a shift. You didn't bother with sick notes, well, it depended on your doctor whether you'd get one. You'd just work an extra shift to make it up if need be.

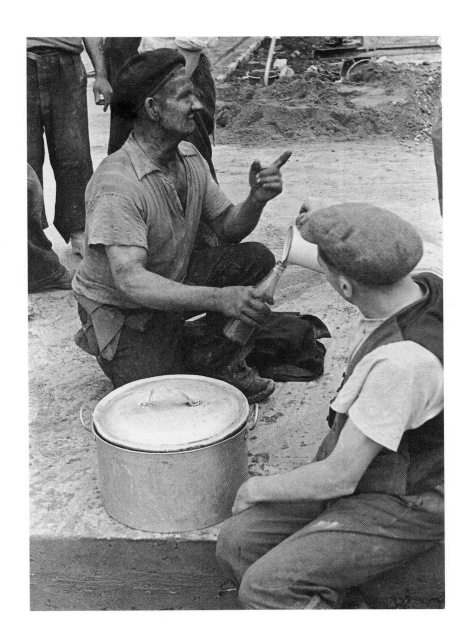

MOST towns round here had big carnival processions. Castleford had one of the best. During the period between the wars the headmaster of the Grammar School was prominent in their organisation.

On one occasion he got miners to dress up as legionaries and ride through the town on pit ponies. They were reckoned to be cohorts moving to Legiolium. That's what they used to call Castleford in Roman times.

MY husband worked in haulage and as a coal miner and also in a storage depot sending out parts for drainage things. It was hard enough work. He started at 7.30am and finished about 5pm.

He would work in the garden too. We had a nice bit of garden with strawberries, blackberries, plums, pears and apples. I used to make jam and sell a lot of it. People would come to the door for that and vegetables too.

There was no need to put out a board or take the stuff to a shop to sell it. When the fruit was ripe on the trees or in the garden people would know there was jam to be had and would come to the house to buy it.

THE Fryston Phantom Face was what built the Miners' Welfare. The pit manager was so keen to get the job started that he told the Coal Board that they were breaking into a new seam when what his office people were doing was creating a reservoir of girders, planks, bricks, mortar, screws and the like with which you could build the Welfare Hall and its grounds.

QUITE a few had greyhounds in the village. There was Marion's Pet – she was called Porkie – and Jenny, who on the track was called whispers. Lassie, I remember, was killed out training when a stake which they tied the horses to went through her throat. She was going so fast, you see.

I remember the housing shortage. And the first big political clashes after the war were about squatters. This became a big political issue. One way of measuring a government was how many houses it built by the end of the year – it would be a big voting point for them.

Prefabs were put up from early 1946 onwards as emergency housing until the building programme caught up with demand.

They were only supposed to be up 15 years. There are still people living in them.

THE television brought the crowning of the Queen into our homes.

Now it is taken for granted but then people opened their homes to those who had no television. The kids were given priority and could sit on the floor in front of the set, then it would go up in tiers depending on ages.

I had to help with the baking in our backs, between School Street and North Street. I didn't see much of the fun as I was collecting food and baking it. I made three hundred and fifty buns and the same number of tarts.

Everybody gave something, what a feed we all had that day! Tables were set out in the backs with cloths and all. There were paper hats and games for the kids. Grown ups joined in as well.

I was kept busy with my big jug of tea. I went back to fill it up umpteen times that day. Thank God the war was over!

WASHING and mending pit banickers was a terrible job. They'd be nearly stood up with sweat and pit muck.

You needed a pudding basin inside when you were mending them.

THIS is the picture of a happy man. He's got everything a man could desire; a whippet, a fag and a baby boy.

WHEN the mines got nationalised in 1947 the colliery officials ran up a flag to make the point that from there on the pits belonged to the people. Some believed them.

There was no change in working procedure and no alterations underground.

Things take a long time to change. It wasn't until 1970 that miners were x-rayed to find out the effects of coal dust on the lungs; pneumoconiosis they call it. I've got 40% pneumoconiosis.

PEOPLE got together and arranged carnivals. We dressed the kiddies up and they paraded round the streets.

I remember when Christine was five, she was dressed up as a fairy, she came home excited with her bag of treats.

Before we had the Welfare, dances were held in the pit canteen. We had dancing round the Bullring on VE Night.

We must have had some good dancers in Fryston then.

EZRA Taylor was Castleford's first mayor as well as being the landlord of The Ship on Aire Street, although he was a teetotaller himself.

His great passion was educational work and he was on the board of Governors at Castleford Grammar School.

When there was a do on at the school he'd go round the food tables looking at the jam tarts and say, 'I don't want a tart unless they're really brown.'

Castleford's motto was 'Floreat Legiolium' – Let Castleford Thrive.

PEOPLE were always dressing up. Jack once got arrested for playing Charlie Chaplin. We'd a day off from the pit and we went over Brotherton way with some girls. There were a bit of skylarking then suddenly this policeman appeared and summonsed Jack for causing an obstruction.

He had to appear before Knottingley magistrates. When it got to the bit describing him, Jack was incensed.

'The accused was wearing a false moustache, Your Worship.'

'I wasn't,' said Jack.

'You were,' said the copper.

'We always believe our constables,' ruled the magistrate.

'It wasn't a false moustache.'

'What was it then?'

'A clipping from a peg rug.'

They fined him ten shillings and asked him who he was with. He said he was by himself. We all clubbed together to pay the fine and Jack ended up three shillings better off!

I learned to swim in Fryston Basin. This particular Sunday we went off to the bridge to jump off. I couldn't swim and they used to drag me along on a rope. Well, this day I forgot the rope but one of them said not to worry because this was the day I would learn.

When I jumped off I aimed for the bit by the bank but missed it completely and landed in a deep part. It took six of them to get me out.

The following Wednesday I was on my way back to work at dinner time when I met old Mrs Jolliffe. 'We'd have been putting you away today,' she said. I thought, 'That's a nice thing to say.'

I went without many times to make sure my kids had enough food. I never went for a night out when my children were little. I stayed with them always. I still say those were the good old days. Neighbours were neighbours, you helped each other.

Perhaps I think this because I was young then. Times were hard but you always managed a chat and a laugh over the fence.

MEN liked big dogs. They still do. This one from what I remember was a killer who had done for several others in dog fights.

Staffordshire Bull Terriers were popular but then this village was populated by Staffordshire people. They came up when the pit first opened.

We were fed Staffordshire oatcakes and even when the bosses wanted soldiers to fire on a crowd they sent for the Staffordshire Regiment. That happened in Featherstone in 1893.

WE'D set piles of bricks up in the street and take turns jumping over.

Often you'd be jumping nearly your own height and it was on concrete so you'd no soft landing on the other side.

THE V.E. Day celebrations also marked the end of the need for the air raid shelters which hadn't been used much anyway because people preferred to make it into the open.

'They've dropped the little shit,' this mister said as they went across the pub hill. He meant flares and incendiary bombs. 'The big shit will be coming soon.'

'Don't go on about that,' his wife replied, 'first watch out for the hoss shit.'

One woman wouldn't leave the house without her false teeth. 'Don't be a silly bugger,' her husband shouted up to her, 'they're dropping land mines not bloody pork pies.'

An old woman who lived down our street was well looked after. At midday Mother would send either my sister or me with her dinner and ten minutes later we took her pudding.

Each evening one or the other of us sat with her to play dominoes or cards. I quite enjoyed those evenings although I was only eight or nine years old.

The only thing that used to upset me was when the old lady went over to the kitchen sink and vomited into an old pint pot. My stomach used to heave and I would make any excuse to dash off home.

GILLIGAN's roundabout came on Friday. If you had a penny that would get you a ride but what they were most keen on was jam jars and rags. When I was a kid I once took my father's shirt out, still in the cellophane.

'Does your dad know you've got this?' Mrs Gilligan asked. 'Yes, of course,' I answered. 'Go and ask him again,' she said. I reckoned to but when I got back they had gone.

Later, when I had got kids of my own, I emptied two bottles of jam into pudding basins so they could have something to take to get a ride.

THE Picture Post and The Illustrated were where you saw good photography in those days. Both papers died when television came along.

The most famous photographer working for the Post was Bert Hardy. He took that picture of the two girls sitting on the front at Blackpool with the wind blowing up the one's dress so that you can see her knickers. She was reckoned to be from Featherstone.

I had a young aunt who wanted to leave her parents, my grandparents, to get married. So when I was fifteen I went to look after my gran and grandad. They had nineteen children. I did the washing, cleaning and baking. Grandad taught me how to make bread.

My aunt had become tired of all the children. When she went to work away, she said she would only stay with a family until they had children.

FRYSTON Welfare was something to be proud of. Some will tell you that it was built OBE – built on Other Buggers' Efforts. They'll say that it was no more than a place where men would meet together to drink, play dominoes and darts.

That's selling it a bit cheap. There were murals, processions and the like. For a brief period it brought the community together.

OUR gillin 'oil in School Street was similar to this in Wellington Street although from what I remember theirs was filled with ashes whereas ours led on to the toilets.

In our part of the village people had to share whereas up the other end people had their own.

We shared with Charlie Pop and Annie. They had about thirty cats so when I wanted to go I would run back to my brothers.

THE village bobby once said to my dad, 'It's not the live ones who give me the trouble, it's the dead ones.' There was always someone drowning themselves in the Aire.

Once my little un came up and said, 'There's a man up there saying he's going to throw himself in the river.' I thought she was joking and said, 'Tell him it'll be cold.' A bit later he floated by. 'Bloody hell,' I thought, 'he meant it.'

We tried to get him out with one of those poles you use to lift up school windows but then a line of Tom Puddings came by and he was sucked under the leading one.

USUALLY the allotments were the man's domain but my mother also got involved with ours. She revelled in paddling around barefoot in all the muck. Dad, for his part, did the spade work.

She died at 77 but had the most beautiful feet I've ever seen, not one corn or bunion. She put it down to paddling around in duck shit for years.

WE had two sons and my husband vowed they'd never go down the mine. That was fine by me. I could remember my dad coming in from the pit. I used to sit and cut up a rubber ball in two to tie round his knees because he had to crawl so far underground those days. The pits were privately owned then.

One day I was sitting looking out of the window and I saw a mister coming to our house. You said mister in them days because you had to be polite. The man opened our door and just said to my mam, 'They've taken him to Pinderfields, he's had nobbut two toes off.' That's how he told us my dad had had an accident at work.

MY brother, a merchant seaman, bought Amber for me. She was the best dog I ever had. Standing on that wall with Mrs Hunter and Victor is typical. She would stay on that wall for hours.

IT meant a lot to us lasses to look smart and to say we didn't have the advanced tackle they have now we did a good job with our hairstyles.

Some women even went shopping in rollers, especially if we had a date on Saturday night, then they were left in all day. I did it myself sometimes.

We kept our hairdos in place with lacquer which stiffened it like board. It contained shell and it was bad to breathe in but there wasn't owt else to use. We tried sugar and water too but that was too sticky.

WOMEN's role altered during the First World War but changed even more dramatically in the second one.

Through conscription, women who were eighteen years old and above had to either join the armed services, the Women's Land Army, nursing, or take up work which had been reserved for men. Bus conductors were replaced by conductresses.

Women who had large families had to act as child minders so that neighbours could be available for work in the munitions factories such as the one at Thorpe Arch, Wetherby. Older women with grown up children worked in the pit canteen or in shops. After the war women continued to work.

THE kitchen was the heart of family life; living room, laundry, dining room, bathroom, and in the winter when babies were due to be born, delivery room. Babies were born into the heart of the family and were very much loved and welcome no matter what the size of the family. My mother maintained that the bigger the family the more love there was to go round.

The kitchen was also a classroom. There we learned to read and write, to cook and bake and, best of all, we learned about life from the stories Dad would tell us. We were weaned on socialism. Now people live in detached houses and lead detached lives.

When we lived in Smith Street the people who had had the house before us had got rid of the old black leaded range, so we advertised for one in The Yorkshire Post and got one for £100. It made lovely Yorkshire puddings. That was only a couple of years ago.

WE used soap a lot. Sunlight, Wheatsheaf – that was green from the Co-op – and long bars of common soap about a foot long for washing floors. White Windsor, that was posh toilet soap, and of course Carbolic – that was red soap for floors and smelt bad.

A young fellow I know went away from home and wrote to his mother, 'If you send me scented soap, make sure it's not Carbolic.'

THE two old men you see guarding the barrel are Tubber Stockdale and Chicker Hulme. Chicker was Jack Hulme's uncle and old Tubber had been an international soccer player for England.

A lot of sportsmen came from Fryston. There was Bill Renton, a Rugby International, Frank Moore played for Featherstone, Arthur Fletcher went to Wakefield Trinity and Joe Anderson to Castleford.

In the old days they used to say that you could shout down a pit shaft and get a prop forward. Where can you go now – Rowntrees?

MY husband loved to cycle, he was in a cycle club from being a teenager. He won all sorts of prizes. One of the things he won was a set of carvers. He was so proud of these he took me to let me have a look at them. When he opened the box it was empty. He shouted to his mother to ask where they were and after a bit of humming and haa-ing she confessed; she had taken them down to the pawn shop.

BEFORE we had the television, the radio provided family entertainment.

There were some great shows. I used to listen to Housewives' Choice.

There was one presenter, George Elrick, a Scottish man, who used to sing along with the theme tune 'I'll be with you again tomorrow morning,' and would sign himself off by saying 'This is Mrs Elrick's wee son George.'

GEORGE Wagstaff was known as Boy because he greeted everyone by saying 'Na boy!' He always had dogs, his signature tune was 'It's the worst bloody dog I've ever had, it won't do nothing!' He said that about every dog he owned.

He had two dogs called Captain and Boy who put him in hospital twice. The first time, he was bragging that he never had to lock his door because the dogs wouldn't let anybody into the house.

He decided to prove it by trying to sneak in the house himself. He crept up the steps, through the door, and Boy slammed into him, knocked him back down the steps and he had to have five stitches in his wrist.

Another time, to prove how loyal Captain and Boy were, he threw himself fully clothed into the river and started splashing about shouting, 'Help Captain, help Boy, I'm drowning!' The dogs jumped into the river, grabbed an arm each and pulled him out. So it was back to the hospital for more stitches.

WHEN I was about ten years old, Grandad decided to put a proper bath in our kitchen. I guess he was one of the first DIY men.

This bath was old, he must have got it from a scrap merchant, but he painted it, inside and out, with enamel paint. We thought we were very posh, fancy having a big bath in our house.

He had made it so that it would empty itself but Mum still had to fill it in the old way. This was great, the only problem was the paint inside the bath soon started peeling and I had to stand there while Mum picked all the bits off my bottom.

OLD lass Morgan laid people out. That's her and her sister.

One of them was very good to Jack. When he fell on the school grating and his knee went wrong it was one of the sisters, not his own mother, who took him day in, day out, by train to Leeds to have it seen to. He reckoned that without her attention he would not have been able to walk.

GEORGE Wagstaff and Mr Baker used to do a double act in the pub, marching up and down the room singing.

The climax of the act was that George vaulted over two or three stools into a somersault but this particular day the box of matches he had in his pocket ignited and set him on fire. Everybody swamped him with ale to put the fire out and the floor of the pub was awash.

Jackie Sharp once left his moped outside the bookie's, well, it was really a henhole that we used as a bookie's.

He'd left it revving on the stand and the lads were having him on shouting 'Hi-ho Silver,' so Jackie took a run and tried to jump on the moped like a cowboy. Of course the inevitable happened, the moped threw him.

WHEN they built the Miners' Welfare they signed the wall and put a bronze bust of a miner over the entrance gate.

They used Scallop as the model. That's him on the right. They poured wax over his face, put straws up his nose and then made a plaster mould.

I don't know what happened to that bust. I suppose somebody whipped it and melted it down, same as happened to the church lead and all the lead markers in the graveyard.

THE Houses of Parliament; that's what they would call it when a lot of men, especially old men, sat on their steps and on the pavement to talk.

You have to remember that in the forties everybody was talking socialism and a better tomorrow. My father, George Henry Owen, for instance, wasn't pink he was crimson.

As a child I can't remember anyone in the village who was a Tory.

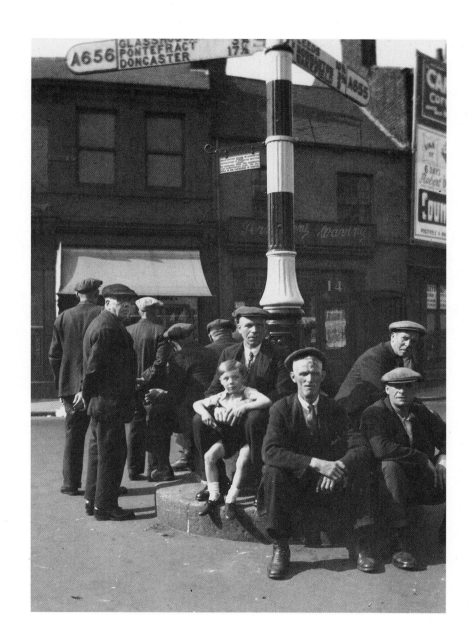

THE old black leaded fireplace was the focal point of the house. On cold nights we'd wrap the oven plate in a cloth and put it to warm the bed instead of a hot water bottle. Dad kept his slippers in the kindling box.

Every week Aunty Maud baked for the whole family, ten loaves and a few scufflers with the dough that was left over. Fresh, hot bread, butter and jam. What a feast! The dough was kneaded in an earthenware bowl, the exact amount put into the loaf tin and into the oven.

Aunty Maud knew from experience how to keep the temperature exactly right to bake the bread by poking and mending the fire regularly.

To clean the chimney some people would stick a firecracker up the flue.

MY brother was a right devil. He once bathed everyone in Vim because it said on the packet 'For everything except clothes.'

Another time he made some custard and complained to Mother that it wouldn't pour. When she looked, he'd made it in the kettle.

THE places round here have grandiose names. There's Ledston Luck, a pit and two rows of houses, Whitwood Mere, a housing estate and Ferrybridge which is a big power station. Then there's Water Fryston, Monk Fryston, Ferry Fryston and just plain Fryston.

I know a young teacher who chose to come north because she saw the name Allerton Bywater. She got a wide awakener. She couldn't see it for two days. Allerton fogs were something to remember.

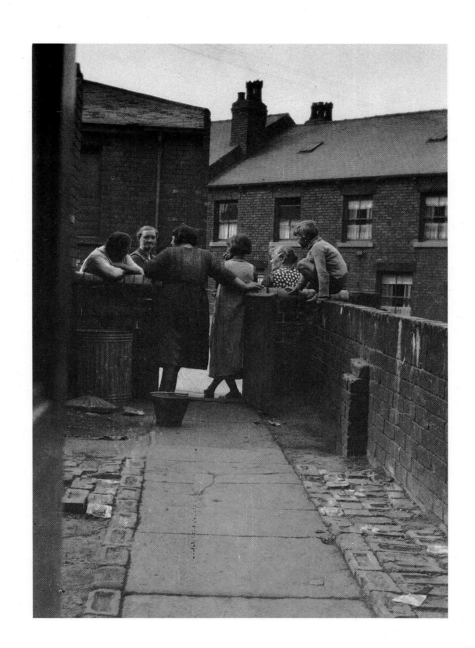

I always went pea pulling in the season with my little stool and bucket. It was good money if you were a fast puller. The first time I went, this old lass shouted me to straighten up every few minutes. I didn't and when I reached the end of the row I couldn't. My back was locked. That taught me a lesson.

The farmer paid us about a penny a peck, which was a bucketful. These went into a sack until it was full. Some crafty devils used to put stones in the sack to make it weigh heavy but the farmer wasn't daft and usually cottoned on. I remember once a farmer said to a man, 'You've been a long time picking a bucketful.'

'It's not the picking that takes the time,' he replied, 'It's the shelling.' He'd a bucketful of shelled peas.

I had a beautiful silk tie. I wish I had it now. It would have to be worth fifty or sixty quid.

White silk scarves were popular then for young men. The older end wore mufflers. Young boys got ties when they went off to secondary school.

MY wife's parents were a close and devoted couple. They even soaked their false teeth together in the same glass. She was large and well built with large teeth. My father-in-law was wiry and tough but five feet four and small made. His teeth were small too so both sets fitted nicely in the same glass, his nestling snugly inside hers.

THERE were always men out dragging for corpses. The River Aire is famous for its suicides.

I am told that they kept an old railway carriage up at the top of the village which acted as a mortuary.

My dad was swimming in the basin one day when he bumped into the corpse of a young woman. Her hair was streaming out behind her. 'I went away like bloody Jesse Owen,' he said.

THAT'S Reg Booth. Him and me used to work for this old miner who would send us for beer in a big screw top bottle. When he wanted more he'd always shout the same. 'Am I on a bloody desert?' Well, this time we were on our way back and got thirsty so we took a drink. When we had finished it was obvious that we had drunk some so we decided to pee into the bottle to top it up.

Half an hour after we had got back we heard him bellow, 'Am I on a bloody desert?' We laughed and laughed.

The Booths lived down the bottom end and Joe Booth was known all over Castleford; he could play anything, though mostly he played wind instruments, piccolo, flute and tin whistle.

I sometimes used to go collecting money for him in The Lion, The Crimea, The Jockey and The Mexborough. He was very tall, just like a sergeant major, and he carried a stick under his arm.

THE Land Army was a healthy alternative to the munition factories. If I remember correctly the best uniform was very smart, consisting of pale khaki with medium tan brogues. They looked wonderful when they came home on leave, bronzed and healthy, while their factory friends working shifts looked pale and tired.

Many got to know German POWs and some romances blossomed, this in spite of the rule that there should be no fraternizing with prisoners.

SOME in Fryston didn't bother putting tablecloths on the tables else when you lifted your pot there would be a ring of dust where it had been. There was that much dust coming from the pit yard we must have eaten more in our houses than we did down the pit.

When Grandmother died they carried her from Oxford Street, Castleford to Fryston Cemetery. By the time they got there the flowers on the top of the coffin were black with coal dust from the pit yard. You never forget things like that.

THE Charles Atlas course which was advertised in the back of most papers, proclaimed 'You too can have a body like mine. Send for the course.' The one in the cossie presumably did.

More modest men would paddle in the shallow water complete with jacket and tie, trouser legs rolled up above their knees. They were the ones who got sand kicked in their faces.

WHEN gas masks were issued at the beginning of the war we had to go to the village school to collect them and be shown how to put them on. We carried our gas masks everywhere, packed in cardboard boxes which hung from a long piece of string. Woe betide anyone who arrived at school without a gas mask.

There was a great apprehension about gas masks. Women in particular were very frightened especially when they had to completely encase young babies in the special gas masks. One woman went into a dead faint when she was issued with hers. Thank God we never had to use them.

LADS weren't any tougher then than they are now, but you'd get the odd big one who'd take advantage. I wasn't a big lad so I did come up against it a bit.

There was one boy who was head and shoulders bigger than me and when we went to the Tech, well, he wasn't right clever and he used to bully others into doing his homework for him. He made me do it once but I reckoned I wouldn't let him get away with it, so I made up lots of daft answers. When he handed it in the teacher in charge took the pump to him – a plimsoll he kept specially on his desk for the job.

I knew I was for it after class so when break came I made a run for it. He was bigger than me and he ran faster and caught me up on the stairs. He picked me up by the collar and hung me over the balcony so I was dangling in the stairwell. I was right terrified. Then he dropped me and I broke an ankle when I fell.

I didn't tell anyone what had happened but someone else did and the lad was suspended for a while. I wasn't big and couldn't run fast so I had to get my own way by slyer methods. I usually managed it somehow.

EVERY year they used to bring the pit ponies up out of the pit and let them run loose in fields down by Fairburn Cut. All the kids used to go to see them and we'd always take a slice of bread to feed them with. They were the fattest pit ponies anywhere!

In 1971 they stopped using the ponies down Fryston pit and as soon as the horses went they bulldozed the fields where they used to graze.

It's funny how people from outside mining areas never think of us living in the countryside yet miners' families are usually in more contact with nature than most.

There was a bloke used to walk to Selby every Sunday morning and come back with a sack full of watercress on his back. The sack would be wet through. He picked the watercress at the side of dykes, it only grew in special places, and he sold it in clumps for happen a halfpenny or a penny a time.

MEN would think nothing of playing games with kids in the street. It could be a real laugh; hordes of us playing circle games with the younger men or someone's dad in the centre.

WOMEN who were depressed lived on aspirins and were said to be suffering with their nerves. No medical condition was very precise.

My mother, for instance, once told me that I had burst a blood vessel in my forehead and had me thinking that there were little vessels of blood held somewhere between the top of my nose and my brain which had been ripped open.

Once I had difficulty in going to the lavatory for what we call a Number One. It hurt and when I told my gran, who I called Mother, she went to see my mother who I called Mam. 'Our Tony tells me,' she said, 'that the roof of his bottom is coming down.'

We come from a long line of colliers.

ALBERT Templeman, Rexy Price, Ronnie Lister and me made a sword apiece and went fencing in the fields. One of the lads threw his sword in the air and it dropped on the electric cables and shorted them out. There was a big flash all along the riverside and the lights went out on the pit top.

We set off and kept running all the way to Fairburn. We thought we'd got away with it but somebody had seen us and gave all our names to the pit manager.

We made our way back to the mate's house and we'd not been in ten minutes before there was a knock at the door. It was Mr Roebuck, the bobby. Our mate's dad said, 'What's up Harry? What have they done?' The bobby said, 'Only put the bloody pit out of action.'

HARRY Mattison was shaftsman at Fryston Pit. He was working one Sunday greasing girders when he must have missed his footing and tumbled straight down the shaft; 550 yards, poor bugger.

I had passed him on the gantry going to work as I left the shift. Nobody knows exactly what happened to this day.

WHEN did you last see a blackclock? Most houses had them when I were young. I'd go into a dark room to light the gas and the gaslight would show walls covered with them. When you put the light on them they'd scurry away to their holes. I was lucky if I killed a couple. Some of the big buggers would blow out your candle if you got near them.

I used to pour boiling water down their holes if I could find them. It didn't seem to work, though, they could swim.

When I was a baby, we lived in my granny's sweet shop and my mam caught me one day eating licorice bits, or so she thought. One of the bits of licorice ran up my arm –I'd been eating blackclocks!

MY mother had some strange remedies which had been passed on by her mother. If I had a sore throat she made a small tube with a piece of paper and put a spoonful of sulphur powder into the end of the tube. Then I had to open my mouth wide and she blew hard down the tube. The powder shot into my throat and took my breath away.

For a bad chest she cut a large piece of brown paper with a big hole in the centre for my head to go through. Then she smeared it liberally with lard and patted it onto my skin. It made a kind of double bib to cover the back and the chest. The paper had to stay on till it disintegrated, about a week, by then the chest cold had usually gone. It was uncomfortable and embarrassing to wear at school because it crackled and rustled when I moved.

ONE of my favourite pals at the pit was deaf and dumb and a good painter. I could always have a good chat with him whilst he was working. He'd shout me over with his arms, waving them like mad. A few words chalked on the wall and a few hand signals and I knew exactly what he was saying.

He always carried a piece of chalk and a wiper. Wherever he was, he always used the same brick, rubbing it clean before writing his next words. He liked a joke and always ended up telling me something funny and laughing with his mouth wide open. A silent laugh.

TURBANS in my day were worn by most young lasses be it for work purposes or, as a lot of us did, for covering a head full of rollers.

Putting on a turban became quite a skill. Some had no idea while others did them really neat. The woolly squares were easy to do but the silky head squares were slippy and rode along your ears so that you were forever pulling it down. It was an arm aching job, for a good head of hair took lots of different sized rollers.

Mind, we considered it was a step up from all-over pin curls. We slept in our hair curlers all night long, spending nearly all night trying to get to sleep. Sometimes I got so mad I sat up at three in the morning taking the buggers out because my head hurt so much and then put the turban back on to keep the remaining curls in place.

WHEN trips were organised the coaches would line up from one end of the village to the other, sometimes as many as thirty. We took sandwiches and flasks, and had very little money to spend.

We might only be going to Roundhay Park but we thought we were leaving the country.

I went to work at the pit – same as most kids. It was dreadful working under private enterprise. You were too tired to go out when you got home. I did pony driving at first. You had to take tubs of coal out from the face. We had some favourites in the ponies and there were some we didn't like.

They came straight from Wales or Russia and we had to break them in. We just used to walk them up and down and talk to them and they got tame. They'd come when you whistled. They could count. They knew how many tubs they'd got on. If there was one too many they wouldn't budge. But there was more value placed on a pony's life than a miner's or a boy's.

LIKE all the pits round here, Fryston's National Union of Miners had its own silk banner.

Probably the last time it was out was when it led the miners back to work following the 1984-1985 strike and before that at the funeral of Joe Green, the picket from Kellingley, who got killed at Ferrybridge.

WHEN you get older, reminiscing is all a lot of people have left. It seems to keep them happy but we're not all content with that.

I like company and I get lonely like a lot of older people do. Apart from lack of money, loneliness is the worst enemy of old age. It's the cause of depression in a lot of older folk. It's almost like an illness itself: looking at the clock and it never moves, locking the door, opening it, getting the insurance money ready hours before he comes, going to bed out of the way.

LAUNDRY was done in the copper and some women had a little line over the sink where they could put small things to dry. I'll never forget when my mother had some washing knocked into the sink, she said 'I hope it hasn't got wet because it isn't dry yet.'

Cleanliness is next to Godliness. That's what my mother used to say as she scrubbed our necks and cleaned inside our ears. She was very particular about hygiene, both bodily and domestic; as a result her whites were whiter than snow and her coloureds bright and fresh.

The domestic science teacher, Miss Edwards, always used to compliment me and my sister on our crisp white aprons and caps. I used to swell with pride when she used mine as an example of how everyone else should look. I took a delight in passing her words of praise on to Mother when I got home.

WHEN Horace Crossley got buried under a fall of roof down the pit and broke his back the entire village put the money together to buy him the invalid carriage.

When it arrived it caused a sensation.

THERE were no thoughts or ideas of girls going into further education – just the idea of girls taking exams was seen as a waste of time.

Girls generally went to school, got a job, got married and had kids. That was the overall thought at the time.

THAT'S the top workshop gang on the day that the second diesel went down the pit. It would be about 1941. The first one was smaller and called Oscar after Oscar Fisher, the manager.

I didn't work with this lot but in the fitting shop. What an experience. When Mr Sutcliffe entered apprentices were required to say, 'Good morning, Mr Sutcliffe.'

It was always Mister, never Benny. If you didn't it was head first into a butt of oily water. Once I made a mistake and they put a piece of metal through my coat sleeves and hoisted me up on a crane and left me hanging there.

When you look back to those days it's hard to remember that since they closed down Wheldale last year hardly anyone in Airedale or Fryston works in the pits. Glasshoughton, Fryston and Wheldale, all of Castleford's pits gone; nothing to see.

Some still have jobs at The Prince in Pontefract and at Allerton Bywater, but the majority have to travel into the Selby coalfield, thirty miles there and back. You need a car to do that.

THE underground miners took to the showers very well as they were used to stripping off below ground in hot conditions but some surface workers were rather shy and covered themselves with their towels.

At Fryston Pit a loincloth was provided because it was illegal to be naked in the showers and a five pound fine was imposed on offenders. This was not the general rule, although at most pits men came in at first wearing bathing costumes. In the 60s the cubicles were removed, except for maybe two in each bay.

Some wouldn't wash the muck off their backs because they thought it weakened them but you never heard much about strong black backs after the showers came in.

EVERY time we saw him coming down the road we'd sing:

> *Okie Pokie penny a lump*
> *That's the way to make you jump*

That's what we would sing but the lads would say, 'trump.' The freezer box was attached to a tricycle and we didn't consider it to be good ice cream unless it had lumps of ice in.

Eldor comes from Eldorado, the city of gold. When you think of it the ice cream was a sort of yellow colour. You don't get proper ice cream today.

ACCIDENTS occurred every day at the pit, the men just seemed to take them for granted. One bloke I remember went into the pit yard just as his brother was being brought out of the pit en route for the hospital where his leg was amputated.

Later, their youngest brother, Percy, also lost a leg. When he told this story he would often remark, 'Wooden legs seemed to run in our family!'

THE streets were our playgrounds. On Shrove Tuesday
we would sing:

> *Pancake day, shuttlecock day,*
> *If you don't give a penny,*
> *We won't go away.*

Mischief Night, the night before Bonfire Night, was
another time we asked for money.

JACK said 'When they take down the Fryston headgear it will be like taking the crown from the King's head.'

The pit closed soon after the 1984/5 strike ended. On a warm, sunny day in June 1987 British Coal blew up the old wheels. There was a large crowd with British and German TV crews – Jack's exhibitions guaranteed that.

When the charges went up at 8 o'clock nothing happened. The whole crowd burst into laughter. In the end it took them two hours and a pile more explosive to topple it.

Where the pit once stood there is an ungrassed field.